essential careers™

CAREERS IN
RESTAURANTS

SIMONE PAYMENT

ROSEN
PUBLISHING®

Published in 2014 by The Rosen Publishing Group, Inc.
29 East 21st Street, New York, NY 10010

Copyright © 2014 by The Rosen Publishing Group, Inc.

First Edition

Library of Congress Cataloging-in-Publication Data

Payment, Simone.
Careers in restaurants/Simone Payment.—First edition.
    pages cm.—(Essential careers)
Includes bibliographical references and index.
ISBN 978-1-4488-9475-8 (library binding)
1. Restraurants—Vocational guidance—Juvenile literature. 2. Cooks—Juvenile literature. 3. Food service employees—Juvenile literature. I. Title.
TX945.P357 2014
647.95023—dc23

2012039555

Manufactured in the United States of America

CPSIA Compliance Information: Batch #S13YA: For further information, contact Rosen Publishing, New York, New York, at 1-800-237-9932.

contents

INTRO

Part of a server's job can be to create a fun dining experience. This server is preparing Bananas Foster at a restaurant in the French Quarter of New Orleans.

DUCTION

W hether the economy is strong or weak, people always need to eat. That's the main reason a job in a restaurant is often a secure one, even in a bad economy. Even when people have less money to spend on entertainment or vacations, they might at least have enough to go out to eat at a favorite restaurant.

In the United States, the restaurant industry is the second largest employer in the private sector. (The private sector refers to jobs that are not part of the U.S. government or the military.) In fact, one out of every ten people who work in the private sector is employed in the restaurant industry.

In recent years, the restaurant industry has continued to grow, even during uncertain economic times. The National Restaurant Association and other industry groups predict that the growth will only continue in the coming years.

The fact that the restaurant and food service industry will continue to grow is one good reason to consider a career in the field. However, there are many other reasons to consider a career in a food-related profession. For one thing, it is an industry in which it is possible to advance from an entry-level job to the very top of the profession, without necessarily having any formal training. For example, someone who begins with an after-school job as a dishwasher can eventually work up through the ranks to become a head chef. However, it takes hard work, dedication, and a willingness to learn.

Most restaurant and food service jobs require the same general qualities. Enthusiasm, energy, and a willingness to work hard are some necessary traits for succeeding in the restaurant industry. Most jobs also require an ability to work well with other people—both with customers and with coworkers. The ability to stay calm under pressure or in chaotic situations is also important. Having a good attitude and a willingness to take direction and learn from others are also good traits for restaurant industry workers. Of course, a love of food can't hurt!

There are many positives to a job in the food service industry. Restaurant jobs provide workers with the opportunity to do something positive in the form of feeding people and making others happy. Most restaurant jobs are very fast-paced, so a workday often goes by very quickly. Restaurant jobs can also be a lot of fun, particularly for those who love food or enjoy being around other people. Some restaurant jobs allow for a great deal of creativity.

Although there are plenty of positives, there are some drawbacks to a career in the restaurant industry. Most jobs require long hours, and many are physically demanding. Some jobs even involve a certain amount of physical danger. For example, chefs may get cuts or burns during a shift. Servers may be injured in falls or get cuts or bruises. However, most drawbacks are minor and are outweighed by the many positive aspects of working in the restaurant industry.

chapter 1

AN OVERVIEW OF THE RESTAURANT INDUSTRY

Anyone interested in working in the restaurant industry will find a variety of careers from which to choose. Most jobs are divided into two categories. The first category involves the people who work behind the scenes in the kitchen. This area is known as the "back of the house" in most restaurants. The other category of worker operates in "front-of-the-house" jobs. These jobs are in the dining room or other outer areas of the restaurant. In general, behind-the-scenes jobs are for those who love food and cooking. These jobs require workers to get along with their coworkers. However, they don't include as much interaction with the public.

Back-of-the-house jobs include chefs and cooks, assistants, and dishwashers. There are several types of chefs, and there may be many types of assistants as well. Restaurants vary in how they set up their kitchen workers and in how many workers they have. Some smaller restaurants, coffee shops, or diners may have just a few chefs. Each chef in a small restaurant may perform many different tasks and do his or her own preparations and cleanup. Other restaurants have a large staff, and each member of the staff may specialize in just one area. For example, a large restaurant or hotel might have a chef who only grills meat or fish and another who only makes desserts.

There are other types of back-of-the-house jobs for people who don't necessarily enjoy cooking. For example, owners or

NOT JUST RESTAURANTS

Working in the food industry doesn't necessarily mean working in a restaurant. There are many places to work other than restaurants. For example, many institutions have cafeterias, including schools, hospitals, office buildings, nursing homes, military bases, and museums. Most hotels include restaurants, and some hotels have several different types of restaurants, from small coffee shops to fine dining. Cruise ships or resorts often have multiple types of places to eat. Dining establishments can also be found at amusement parks and sports arenas. Food is even served from small trucks that travel around a city serving food or park at office parks at lunchtime to serve workers.

managers handle the business details such as paying employees, ordering food, and making schedules. Some restaurants, particularly larger restaurants or chain restaurants, have human resources managers. These workers hire and fire employees, take care of payroll, and create and enforce rules and regulations. In smaller restaurants, the owner or general manager usually handles these tasks.

For people who like food and enjoy working with and helping others, a job in a restaurant as a server or bartender could be fun. Other front-of-the-house jobs include host/hostess, busser, and dining room manager. These jobs all require excellent people skills.

EDUCATION REQUIREMENTS

Some jobs in the restaurant industry require a particular degree, but many do not. There are many paths to a restaurant career. Some people choose to begin working in a restaurant during or just after high school. Many entry-level jobs, such as a dishwasher or server, do not have any

Many restaurant jobs require workers to keep a clear head, such as this hostess who is keeping track of patrons waiting at a busy Denny's restaurant.

education requirements. These types of jobs just require a willingness to work hard. Skills and tasks for these types of positions can be learned on the job. Success in these entry-level jobs can then lead to higher positions, such as prep cook or head server.

OTHER FOOD JOBS

For those people who love food but don't want to cook it or serve it, there are many other food-related careers to consider, including farming. People who like to write might consider food writing, restaurant reviewing, or cookbook writing. Some people specialize in doing public relations for restaurants or food shops. Designers who like food can design restaurant interiors or menus or could try floral arranging. There are photographers who specialize in taking pictures of food for magazines, cookbooks, or promotional materials. Others, called food stylists, specialize in making food look its best for photographs. Nutritionists and dietitians help people make healthy food choices.

For some restaurant positions, some education specific to the career is a good idea. For example, most chef positions require not only experience but some culinary education. At a culinary school, students learn many specific aspects of cooking, such as how to handle a knife and how to bake bread.

How and where a culinary education is obtained can vary. Some people go straight from high school to culinary school. Others work for a year or more, then go to culinary school. Still others attend a culinary arts program at a community college.

Most culinary schools offer hands-on experience in restaurants. For those students who already have experience, some schools offer a shorter program that gives students credit for prior experience.

There are many different types of culinary schools. Some offer programs that last about six months. Other programs last three or more years. Culinary schools can be found all across the United States and in many other countries.

At culinary school, students learn not only how to cook food, but also how to present it in an appealing way.

Schools vary in size and reputation and the types of programs offered. Attending a culinary arts program at a community college can be an advantage because these colleges offer other types of classes, such as business or languages.

Many people in the restaurant industry recommend doing an internship in a kitchen or restaurant before attending culinary school. Some real-world experience can provide a good idea of what working in the restaurant industry is really like. This can ensure that a career in the restaurant industry is the right one to pursue.

Although some restaurant workers suggest not attending culinary school immediately after high school, there are some good reasons to attend culinary school at some point. It provides the chance to learn good cooking techniques, such as how to grill a steak, chop an onion, or make a soufflé. In a busy kitchen, there may not be much time to learn. Also, other workers often don't have extra time to teach someone new. Another advantage of attending a culinary school is that many schools offer help to graduating students looking for jobs.

chapter 2

CHEFS

There are many different types of chefs, and they work in various types of dining establishments. Whether working in a fast-food chain or a high-end restaurant, the basic job description is that a chef cooks food. For some cooking positions, especially entry-level jobs, little experience is necessary to get started. Top-level jobs require years of on-the-job training and a degree from a culinary school.

Some chef jobs allow for a lot of creativity. Chefs in high-level positions get to create the items that appear on the menu of the restaurant. These chefs then cook those dishes or supervise others who do. They choose what ingredients will be included in a dish and where those ingredients will come from. High-level chefs also decide how the dishes will be presented. For example, a chef might select which herbs and seasonings will be sprinkled on top of a meal.

Some chefs do all the cooking themselves, and others supervise the cooking of chefs who work for them. Chefs in lower-level positions may have fewer chances to be creative. Their jobs may be to simply do the work their boss assigns. Some lower-level chefs do only one type of task. For example, some might only cook pasta. Other lower-level chefs perform many different duties during a single shift.

Most chef positions are very rewarding and are perfect for people who are passionate about food. However, most chefs

Cooking is a very portable career—it is possible to get a job almost anywhere, such as in Las Vegas, where this chef works.

put in long hours of work. Many chefs don't work a regular schedule of Monday through Friday during daytime hours. This is because most restaurants are open at night and on the weekends, when people most often go out to eat. So working nights and weekends may be a common requirement. Often a chef's shift begins in the afternoon and continues until after midnight.

Some chefs do have the opportunity to work daytime hours at coffee shops, diners, chain restaurants, and cafeterias. Others might work overnight or early-morning shifts at all-night diners or breakfast spots. Most chefs, whatever their job, work long hours.

Cooking is also generally a busy and sometimes stressful job. Chefs have to juggle many different orders at the same time. Servers may give the chef orders from many tables at the same time. Each table may have multiple diners. And each dish for a single customer can have several components, all with different cooking times and needs.

For example, a single order might include grilled fish with sauce, whipped potatoes, and vegetables. The chef must make sure every component for each dish, diner, and table is ready at about the same time so that the orders can be taken to the table while they are still warm. Juggling all these orders takes a good memory and an ability to keep track of many small details. It helps to have good hand-eye coordination.

Kitchens are often hot, with the potential for burns and cuts, or falls on slippery floors. However, most chefs are willing to overlook these drawbacks because they love to cook.

JOB DESCRIPTION

Because there are many types of chefs, the job description for a chef varies widely. Also, each restaurant or dining establishment might have one, or many, chefs. In a particular restaurant,

A chef's main goal is to make food that patrons will enjoy. Some chefs spend time talking to customers during their meal to get feedback or to make suggestions.

every chef might have just one job to do, or he or she might have several different duties.

Some of the many types of chefs include: short-order cook, prep cook, line cook, sous chef, banquet chef, executive chef, and private chef. A short-order cook usually works in a fast-food restaurant, diner, or chain restaurant. These cooks are called "short order" because the meals they prepare do not take long and are fairly simple.

Short-order cooks' job duties include preparing the food for cooking. For example, they might chop vegetables for salads, form ground beef into hamburger patties, or make pancake batter. Then they cook food when orders come in from servers.

A prep cook is an entry-level position. Prep cooks chop, peel, and do other tasks to prepare food for cooking. Prep cooks might slice meat for sandwiches, peel potatoes, or chop vegetables for a soup. Prep cooks usually work during the day or late afternoon, before the kitchen begins preparing meals. Some stay during mealtimes to help other cooks.

Prep cooks work in restaurants, but they may also work in other types of dining establishments. Some examples might include grocery stores, sandwich shops, bakeries, or school cafeterias. Prep cooks may work full-time, but some work part-time.

A line cook works in one particular area of the kitchen. A line cook is sometimes called a station cook or a chef de partie. Line chef duties vary by restaurant or type of restaurant. Usually a line cook is responsible for one particular food item or type of food. For example, a line cook may prepare all pasta dishes. Or he or she may grill any orders of meat, chicken, or fish.

Some line cooks work in groups, especially in a busy station, such as the grilling station. Others may be the only cook at a particular station. Line cooks usually work in large or busy restaurants. Most line cooks work full-time and work the hours before, during, and after a restaurant is open.

Sous chefs supervise other chefs working in the kitchen. In a large, busy kitchen, sous chefs oversee the line cooks. They also coordinate the work of other cooks. A sous chef would

While many chefs work late into the night, others start their day early, working a breakfast shift at a busy diner or truck stop.

make sure the grill cook, pasta cook, and vegetable cook have all the parts of a meal ready at the same time. Sous chefs may also work as assistants to an executive chef. The sous chef may help the executive chef order food, schedule kitchen workers, or train the staff. A sous chef may also take over for the executive chef if he or she is on vacation or taking a day off.

Banquet chefs work in large restaurants, hotels, or other locations where special events (such as weddings) are held. These types of chefs must prepare meals for large groups. The challenge of a banquet chef is to have dozens, or even hundreds, of meals ready at the same time. A banquet chef usually oversees a team of other chefs.

An executive chef is the highest position in a restaurant kitchen. An executive chef usually creates the menu for a particular restaurant. He or she must make sure to include many different options on the menu. Some restaurants may focus on a particular type of food, such as seafood. But most menus include a wide variety of items that appeal to everyone, including people with allergies or other dietary requirements. Executive chefs order all the ingredients that go into each dish on the menu. An executive chef also supervises other chefs in the kitchen. He or she may

CHEF PROFILE: MARCUS SAMUELSSON

Marcus Samuelsson was born in Ethiopia in 1970 but was adopted and moved to Sweden when his mother died when he was three years old. He began cooking with his grandmother when he was only six years old and knew almost right away that he wanted to be a cook. He went to culinary school in Sweden, Switzerland, France, and Austria.

Samuelsson then moved to New York City to do an internship. He quickly worked his way up to executive chef at a top New York restaurant. He has received many awards for his cooking, has written for newspapers and cooking magazines, and has appeared on several television shows. Samuelsson has even cooked a meal at the White House.

also teach the other chefs how to prepare and cook each dish on the menu.

Private chefs don't work in restaurants. Instead, they work for a family in their home. These chefs prepare all of a family's meals, either at mealtime or ahead of time. Some private chefs are on call at all hours. Others work specific hours and may leave meals in the refrigerator or freezer for customers' mealtimes. Some private chefs even work on private planes or on yachts. Private chefs may also work for multiple families, delivering all their meals for the week.

All types of chefs need to know some basic tasks. They must know how to quickly—and safely—chop, peel, and prepare ingredients. They must know the many different ways to cook food, such as frying, grilling, sautéing, and boiling. All types of

This chef de partie is preparing a dish in the busy kitchen on board the Queen Mary 2, *a luxury ocean liner.*

chefs must know basic food safety. For example, meat must be kept refrigerated, and all items in the kitchen must be kept as clean as possible.

JOB PREPARATION

A good way to begin preparing for any job as a chef is to volunteer in the kitchen at a shelter, retirement home, or school. This can provide an idea of how a large kitchen operates and what being a chef is like. It can also be a good introduction to the many different tasks that a chef might perform.

Most restaurant kitchens have high-powered, high-temperature dishwashing equipment to help keep up with the many dishes, pots, and utensils used by the kitchen staff and diners.

OTHER "BACK-OF-THE-HOUSE" JOBS

In addition to the many chef positions, there are other types of workers in the kitchen. Some large restaurants may hire a butcher to prepare all of their meat. Butchers take large pieces of meat and cut them into smaller portions for individual meals. For example, a butcher may take a whole cow and turn it in to various cuts of meat like T-bone steaks and hamburger.

Another essential back-of-the-house job is dishwasher. Almost every kitchen hires one or more people to clean all of the dishes, silverware, pots, pans, and glasses used by the chefs and the diners. Most kitchens have one or more automatic dishwashers, but some delicate items like wine glasses or cooking equipment need to be washed by hand.

Getting an after-school job at a fast-food restaurant or in the kitchen of any other type of restaurant can also provide an idea of what it is like to work as a cook. Even working as a dishwasher or prep cook provides a chance to observe what the life of a chef is like. Working at the deli counter of a supermarket is another option. Slicing meats and making salads and other prepared foods can provide a good cooking background.

Learn basic skills like how to use different types of knives. Some after-school or community education programs offer classes that teach basic cooking skills. Some high schools or vocational schools offer culinary programs. Take advantage of these opportunities to begin building a career.

Chefs don't always work in a busy kitchen. This personal chef is preparing a salad in a customer's home kitchen.

Studying a second language can be helpful for a career in a kitchen. Food workers come from different countries. Spanish and French are especially helpful.

Prep cooks and line cooks don't usually need formal training to begin working in a restaurant or other food service location. Most prep and line cooks are trained on the job.

Other types of chefs require experience as well as some formal culinary education. After high school, attending a community college culinary program can be a good next step. These programs help graduates find jobs during and after graduation. If attending community college, taking business classes can be good preparation for the other aspects of some chef positions.

Most culinary schools and community college programs send students to work in restaurants. These jobs are called externships, and they usually last a few months. Even in programs without formal externships, schools recommend that students find jobs in local restaurants to get extra experience. Some culinary schools have on-campus restaurants where students can gain experience.

SALARY AND CAREER ADVANCEMENT

Chefs' salaries vary quite a bit. Salary depends not only on the size and type of restaurant, but also on experience. Smaller restaurants offer lower salaries, particularly to entry-level chefs. Executive chefs with many years of experience working in a high-end restaurant can make a great deal more. These chefs may also be able to make additional money writing cookbooks or making television appearances. For up-to-date salary information, please visit the Web site of the U.S. Bureau of Labor Statistics.

Some chefs choose to start their own restaurant. An experienced chef could start another small business, such as a specialty food store or catering company. Chefs may also combine cooking with other related skills. For example, a chef might open a bed and breakfast. A chef might also teach at a cooking school or offer private cooking lessons.

There are plenty of opportunities for career advancement for chefs. With experience, entry-level prep cooks can move up within a restaurant. It is also possible to move to a new restaurant for career advancement. High-level chefs can also work in a restaurant in a foreign country.

chapter 3

Pastry Chefs and Bakers

P astry chefs and bakers make all kinds of desserts and breads. In some restaurants or shops, one person creates both types of baked goods. In other places, the two jobs are separate. In that case, bakers usually make things like breads, rolls, and muffins. Pastry chefs make cakes, pies, tarts, cookies, ice cream, candy, and many other desserts. Sometimes there is some overlap, even when the two jobs are separate. For example, both the baker and pastry chef may make cookies.

Pastry chefs and bakers work in many types of restaurants. They may also work in specialty shops like bakeries, cake shops, or coffee shops. Pastry chefs and bakers could also work in cafeterias or even on cruise ships. Some work in large commercial kitchens that supply baked goods to many different restaurants.

All pastry chefs and bakers need to know how to produce a wide variety of baked goods. They must be able to make basics like bread, cakes, pies, and cookies. They must also be able to create specialized items like tarts or candy, as well as produce individual components that make up some desserts. For example, some desserts are filled with mousse or creams, so bakers and pastry chefs must know how to prepare those ingredients and how to insert these fillings into the filled desserts. Pastry chefs and bakers also make ice cream, sherbet, and gelato.

SPECIALIZED PASTRY CHEFS

In large hotels or restaurants, there may be several pastry chefs, each with a specialty. These specialized pastry chefs are known by French names. The pâtissier is the pastry chef, who makes most of the cakes, pies, tarts, cheesecakes, and other treats. The confiseur makes candy and small cakes or pastries. A décorateur specializes in decorating the desserts made by the pâtissier. The boulanger bakes bread and muffins. The boulanger may also make some pastries, cakes, and cupcakes.

Both jobs require workers who are strong, calm under pressure, and willing to work hard. These jobs also require precision. Unlike cooking, where chefs can experiment with ingredients, pastry chefs and bakers must be exact. They must follow recipes closely and use the correct amount of each ingredient. For example, if a baker does not use enough yeast in the dough, the bread will not rise. If a cake is

not baked long enough, it will be raw in the middle. Therefore, pastry chefs and bakers should be detail-oriented. They should also have good math skills. These come in handy when doubling a recipe, for example.

Some bakeries serve standard items that are always on the menu, such as chocolate chip cookies, but add specialties like gingerbread men during the Christmas season.

These two jobs—particularly pastry chef—allow for some creative skills. Although recipes must be followed to gain the right results, pastry chefs and bakers can experiment with new flavor combinations and new recipes. They can also apply creative skills to make desserts look attractive. They can apply decorative touches like berries. Pastry chefs might also drip

This assistant manager at a bakery in Cambridge, Massachusetts, starts his workday at 1 AM. Additional bakers join him at 3 AM.

sauces and other garnishes on top of desserts in interesting and elaborate patterns that really beautify these dishes.

ON THE JOB

A pastry chef's day usually starts quite early. Often the pastry

chef is the first person in the kitchen every morning. Bakers start early, too, especially those who work in commercial bakeries or small shops. At the beginning of the day, the pastry chef or baker will check to see what is left from the day before. He or she will make a list of what needs to be baked or prepared that day. Because some desserts will stay fresh for several days, not every dessert on the menu will need to be prepared each day. But many desserts and baked goods do need to be made fresh daily.

With a list of items to make in hand, the baker or pastry chef will gather ingredients and begin making each item. While the first baked goods are in the oven, the pastry chef can move on to

A PASTRY CHEF'S CAREER PATH

Yuko Kitazawa is a pastry chef who works at a top restaurant in Los Angeles. She was always interested in baking and cooking and loved making desserts while in high school. She went to college, but knew that what she really wanted to do was be a pastry chef. After graduating from college, she attended the Culinary Institute of America. While at the Culinary Institute, she did an externship at the Four Seasons Hotel in Chicago. With her culinary degree, she began working for caterers and restaurants. Eventually she got her dream job as a pastry chef in a high-end restaurant. There she comes up with new desserts and produces all dessert items for the restaurant.

creating the next item on the list. He or she might make ice cream from scratch or decorate a finished cake.

What the pastry chef or baker makes each day can vary, depending on the menu and what is in stock. A pastry chef working in a restaurant that is open only at night will probably make and decorate several desserts each day. Which desserts are made depend on what is being offered on the menu that day. A small bakery or coffee shop may have a more fixed menu, so bakers there might create the same items each day. Offerings might include breakfast pastries, doughnuts, muffins, bagels, and other baked goods.

JOB PREPARATION

Students who would like to become a pastry chef or baker can start working toward their career any time. One of the best ways to prepare is to just start baking. Work with different ingredients and combinations. Try varying a recipe to see what happens when the proportions or ingredients change.

Volunteering for a nonprofit organization is an informal way of gaining cooking and kitchen experience, with the added benefit of helping other people.

Working an after-school job in a bakery or commercial kitchen can be a great way to get an idea of what the job is all about. Or try volunteering in a soup kitchen or in the kitchen at a retirement home.

After high school, someone interested in pursuing a career as a baker or pastry chef can take several routes. One route is to find a job as an assistant or apprentice baker. Another route is to go to culinary school. Many culinary schools have special-ized baking or pastry chef programs. Many junior or community colleges also have culinary programs for bakers and pastry chefs.

To get most jobs in the pastry and baking field, a degree is not essential. What is more important is experience and good baking skills. However, a degree can help a baker or pastry chef get a better-paying job. Bakers can also get a certification from the Retail Bakers of America. There are four levels of certification, including management, sales, training staff, and cleanliness. Certification is essential for those who want to own their own bakery or retail store.

SALARY AND CAREER ADVANCEMENT

Salaries for pastry chefs and bakers vary, depending on the type of job and location. Assistants or apprentices usually make salaries on the low end. Pastry chefs in fancy restaurants in large cities, or people who own their own stores or bakeries, make top salaries. Once a pastry chef is at the top of the industry, changing jobs is a way to advance.

Some pastry chefs and bakers work part-time in a restaurant and then have a second job working for a caterer or bakery. Some may have a full-time job with a small side business of their own, making wedding cakes, for example.

chapter 4

SERVERS

From small cafés to the most expensive restaurants, servers have the same basic job: help customers have a good dining experience. Servers take customers' orders for food and drinks, give the orders to the kitchen, and then deliver food and drinks to the customers. Some dining establishments, such as fast-food restaurants or cafeterias, don't have servers. But most others do, so there are many job opportunities for servers in a wide range of settings.

Some servers work a fixed schedule, working the same hours every week. Other servers' hours change week to week. These servers may vary the number of hours they work, or the days and times of their shifts. Some servers might work more hours during a busy season, such as during the summer at a restaurant at a vacation resort. Therefore, working as a server can be a great job for people who want to work part-time or who need a flexible schedule.

Servers often work nights and weekends because these are the most popular times for dining. Therefore, being a server can also be a second job for people who have weekday, daytime jobs but would like to earn extra money.

A server's job is very fast-paced, especially in a popular restaurant at a busy time of day. Most servers are trained on the job and don't require any schooling or degree. This is another reason why it is a good first job or part-time job.

Servers are responsible for making sure orders are fulfilled properly and that diners remain happy.

Being a server can be physically demanding, and some shifts can be long and tiring.

Servers are on their feet most of the time and must carry heavy plates or trays of food. Although these can be drawbacks, many servers see them as positives. A busy shift goes by very quickly. With more customers, there are more opportunities to make money. Some servers also enjoy the fast pace of the work.

Being a server is a great job for people who like food and helping other people. Servers need physical strength and a good memory. They need to be pleasant, even on a bad day. They must be efficient and organized and be able to keep a clear head under pressure. Some servers add up a customer's bill at the end of a meal, so good math skills can come in handy.

Being persuasive can also be a helpful attribute for servers. If they are able to talk customers into ordering more food or drinks than the customers had planned, the final bill will be higher. This is good for the restaurant and for the server. This is because servers usually make minimum wage. The rest of their earnings are made up of tips left by customers. Tips are

SERVERS' HELPERS

In some restaurants, especially in large or busy ones, servers may have help from captains, bussers, or runners. Captains are in charge of the servers, planning who works which shifts and overseeing the servers' work. In some cases, a captain may help the servers during an especially busy shift. Bussers help servers by clearing the table during and after a meal. Bussers may also refill customers' water glasses, or coffee or other drinks. Runners take the food orders from the kitchen out to the tables.

usually based on the total bill, so customers who spend more tend to leave larger tips for their server. A standard tip is 15 to 20 percent of the total bill. But servers who are especially pleasant or helpful can be rewarded for their good service with extra money.

JOB DESCRIPTION

In most dining establishments, servers are responsible for a specified area of the dining room. Or a server may wait on a certain number of tables spread throughout the restaurant. At the beginning of a shift, servers make sure all their tables are set and their area is clean. They make sure the supplies they might need are ready and that condiments or other items on the table are full. Before a shift, a server also reviews what is on the menu and learns about any specials being offered that day. In addition, servers need to know if any menu items are not available that day. They must also know what ingredients are in each dish to help customers with allergies or other diet requirements make menu choices. At some restaurants, servers might also be required to know where the vegetables on the menu are grown or where the fish are caught.

When customers arrive, servers greet them and describe any special menu items. They may also answer questions about items on the menu and make suggestions to diners. When the customer is ready, servers take the drink and food order. They also take notes on any special requirements that are requested by the customer.

The servers note how the diners want their food prepared. For example, they must find out how well done a diner would like his or her meat cooked. They also take diners' orders for side dishes and other options, such as the customer's choice of salad dressing.

It is important for servers to know the restaurant's menu well. That way, they can offer suggestions to diners trying to choose their meal.

TAKING ORDERS

How a server takes a customer's order can vary by restaurant or by server. Some servers memorize a customer's order, so they don't

A friendly, positive attitude is important for servers. Diners appreciate being greeted warmly and with a smile and will be more likely to visit the restaurant again.

write anything down as the customer is ordering. This requires an excellent memory, especially if there are many diners at the table or if the diners make complicated orders. Other servers write everything down on order pads, which they then give to the chefs.

Many restaurants have electronic ordering systems. In these restaurants, servers use smartphones, tablet computers, or other electronic devices to take orders. The orders are then transferred automatically to the kitchen, where they come up on a screen.

After the customers' orders are placed, servers give the order to the kitchen. They get drinks from the bartender or pour them themselves. They deliver drinks, appetizers, or salads to the table. When the main meal is ready, servers bring it to the table, remembering which diner at the table ordered which menu item. While diners are eating, servers check with them to find out how the food is and if the customers need anything else. Servers may refill drinks while the diners are eating.

When diners are finished, servers clear all dishes and ask if customers would like dessert or anything else. At the end of the meal, the server adds up the bill and delivers it to the customers.

This touch-screen ordering system sends orders to the kitchen and totals the bill when the diners' meal is finished.

Sometimes servers take customers' money or credit cards to pay the bill. In other restaurants, a host or other employee takes customers' money and makes change. Once the customers have left, the server clears the table and resets it for the next guests.

Servers are responsible for multiple tables, so when the restaurant is full, the server may be very busy. He or she must juggle multiple tables that are at different stages. Customers at one table may be just arriving and will need menus and drinks. At the same time, food for another table may be ready to be delivered. Yet another table of diners might be leaving and their table must be cleared. This is why good organization skills and a clear head can come in handy for servers.

JOB PREPARATION

To prepare for a career as a server, volunteering at a soup kitchen, retirement home, or hospital can help develop good serving and people skills. After-school or summer jobs in fast-food or chain restaurants can also provide experience. Some restaurants hire servers who are still in high school, particularly during busy seasons, so it is possible to get an after-school or summer job as a server. Some servers begin as bussers or runners and learn by watching servers.

Most servers, even those new to the restaurant industry, are trained on the job by other servers or by managers. Servers can watch other employees, especially those who make a lot of tips, to get ideas on how to be a better server. They can observe how successful servers act with customers and what other things these servers do to create a positive experience for diners. Good servers can also provide helpful hints to new servers on how to remember orders and how to keep track of the many details they must keep in their head during a shift.

SALARY AND CAREER ADVANCEMENT

Servers usually make minimum wage. There is a national minimum wage, but some states set a higher minimum wage for workers in that state. Most of a server's earnings usually come from tips. Therefore, how much a server makes varies widely.

Servers who work in a high-end restaurant can make a good deal of money from their tips. This is because the total bill can be quite high, especially when diners order drinks or desserts. However, even servers in small or less expensive restaurants can make a good salary in tips if the restaurant is busy and the server has many customers per shift.

Servers who want to advance their career or make more money can look for a job in a new restaurant. Servers with experience can usually find a new job quite easily.

chapter 5

BARTENDERS AND WINE DIRECTORS

People who make and serve alcoholic and nonalcoholic drinks are called bartenders. Wine directors are a more specialized version of a bartender. They choose the wines served at a particular restaurant. Wine directors are also sometimes called wine stewards or, from French, sommeliers.

Bartenders can work at a bar or other establishment that only serves drinks. They can also work at restaurants that have a bar area where drinks (and sometimes food) are served. Some bartenders work for caterers at large events such as weddings or conferences. Wine directors usually work in high-end restaurants or in bars that specialize in serving wine.

Bartenders must know about all kinds of drinks and how to make them. They memorize drink recipes or know how to find the recipes for unusual drink requests. Bartenders need to know what kind of glasses specific drinks should be in and the correct way to pour certain drinks.

Wine directors are experts who choose all the wines served at a restaurant. Sometimes wine directors help customers pick the right wine to match their meal. They might also teach the restaurant's servers about the wines on the menu so that the servers can make recommendations to customers.

Restaurant sommeliers work closely with the chefs to determine the best wine to pair with all meals on the menu.

An essential requirement for being a bartender is a friendly personality. Being good with people can be an advantage because bartenders make most of their money as tips from customers. The friendlier and more helpful a bartender is, the higher the tip the customer is likely to leave. Although a fun, friendly personality is helpful, bartenders must be serious about their work. Customers are not likely to give a generous tip to a bartender who is friendly but makes them the wrong drink or forgets to bring the check.

The ability to keep a clear head under busy, stressful conditions is another important quality for a bartender to have. Many bars, especially on weekend nights, are very busy. Bartenders must stay calm to keep track of multiple drink orders and serve everyone as quickly as possible.

Bartenders spend most of their shift on their feet and often work for long stretches at a time. Because some bars are open until midnight or later, bartenders' shifts are usually at night and most work weekend nights when bars are busiest. So stamina and good health are other important attributes for a

Bartenders use an assortment of garnishes for drinks. In addition to preparing them, they must know which garnish to pair with which drink.

bartender to have. Most bartenders also write up bills and take customers' money, so good math skills can come in handy for adding up drink prices and making change.

Bartenders also need good judgment. They must know when a customer has had too much alcohol and then calmly but firmly refuse to serve any more drinks. Bartenders also have to be careful to not serve alcohol to any customers who are not of legal drinking age.

Wine directors usually work under less stressful conditions than bartenders. Their work is usually calmer and behind the scenes. Also, they can do some or all of their work when the restaurant or bar is not open.

Job Description

At the beginning of a shift, bartenders check to make sure the bar is fully stocked with liquor, beer, soda, juice, ice, glasses, and garnishes. They also make sure the bar area is clean. Once a shift is under way, bartenders fill drink orders from customers. They pour beer, wine, and nonalcoholic drinks. Bartenders also make mixed drinks, with different types of liquor and juice or soda. Bartenders may also make recommendations if customers are not sure of what they want.

They keep track of who has ordered which drinks so that they can total up the order when the customer is done. If the bar is part of a restaurant, bartenders also fill drink orders from servers. In some bars, food is served, so bartenders sometimes take food orders and deliver food to customers. At the end of a shift, bartenders clean and restock the bar area.

Barbacks are bartenders' assistants. They help the bartender by keeping the bar stocked with liquor, beer, other drinks, ice, glasses, and garnishes like lemons and limes. They change kegs of beer when they are empty. Barbacks also help keep the bar area clean by wiping up spills, mopping the floors, clearing

Part of a bartender's training includes how to use specialized equipment, such as shakers, strainers, blenders, muddlers, and jiggers.

dirty glasses, and emptying trash and recycling bins. They also run glasses and other equipment through the dishwasher. Sometimes barbacks help out by pouring simple drinks like soda or beer.

Wine directors do part of their work before the restaurant or bar is open. This preparation consists of choosing and ordering the various wines that will be on the menu. The wine director researches wines and the particular vineyards where wines are made. They may travel to vineyards to taste wines and learn about the wine-making process.

Wine directors who work in a restaurant will collaborate with the chef to match wines with food items that are on the menu. The wine director orders wine from suppliers and keeps track of what wines are in stock. When supplies are getting low, the wine director orders more.

The wine director usually teaches the servers about each wine on the menu. This includes information on which wine goes best with which menu items. Wine directors also teach servers how to pour different wines, what glasses to use, and whether to serve the wines at room temperature or chilled. In some restaurants, the wine director only chooses the wine and educates the staff. In others, the wine director also helps customers pick the right wines for their meal. The wine director can explain a bit about each choice, such as what country or region the wine is from and what grapes are used to make the wine. Sometimes the wine director will also serve the wine to the diners. Some wine directors organize special dinners or events at restaurants, wine bars, or other locations.

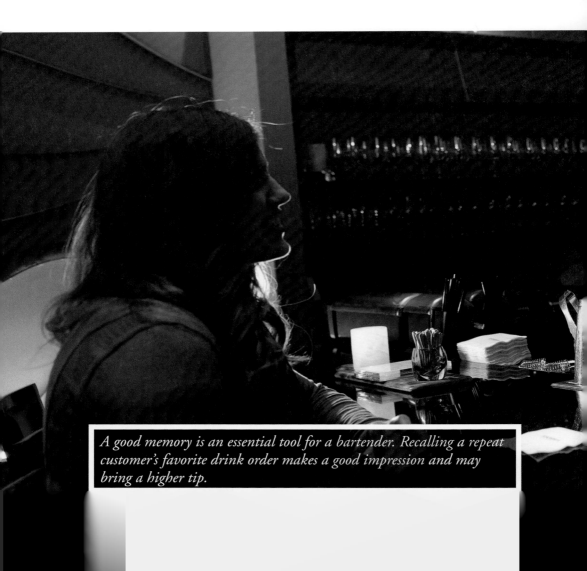

A good memory is an essential tool for a bartender. Recalling a repeat customer's favorite drink order makes a good impression and may bring a higher tip.

JOB PREPARATION

Most bartenders attend bartending school in order to get a job as a bartender. Bartending schools teach students about different types of alcohol, how to mix drinks, which glasses to use, how to pour beer, how to follow recipes, and other necessary bartending skills.

There are many bartending schools from which to choose. Some offer courses that are a few weeks long. Some last only

one night. There are some bartending courses that are offered online. Most of the longer programs will also help graduates find jobs.

Some bartending experience is usually a job requirement. Working as a barback or server can be a good way of gaining experience. Working for a caterer can also be helpful preparation for becoming a bartender. While gaining experience, ask the bartenders questions and observe how they do their job.

Customer service is an essential bartending skill, so potential bartenders should pay special attention to how a successful bartender interacts with customers. Working at other service-oriented jobs can also build customer-service skills. These types of jobs might include working behind the counter at a coffee shop or at a clothing store.

Bartenders can often receive training at a new job. Other bartenders, or managers, will train a new bartender in any specific skills needed to work at that particular restaurant or bar.

In the United States, most states require that anyone serving alcohol be at least eighteen years old. Some states set the age higher. Therefore, bartenders must be at least eighteen years old or older to work in the United States.

Wine directors need more specialized training. There is much to learn about wine, including how and where it is made, how it should be stored, how different wines taste, and what types of wine go with what types of food. Because many wines are made in France and other countries around the world, learning a second language can be helpful.

Some culinary schools offer training programs for wine directors. There are other schools not associated with culinary schools that teach people to become wine experts. Before attending a training program, people who would like to become wine directors could try working at a winery, at a wine shop, or as a server at a wine bar. Learn as much as possible about the many types of wine and how they differ.

After attending a wine program at a culinary school or other organization, people who want to become wine directors can begin working at a restaurant or wine bar. It is also a good idea to become certified by taking a certification exam. Being certified can help a wine director get a better job.

SALARY AND ADVANCEMENT

Like servers, bartenders usually make minimum wage. In addition, they make tips based on the total bill and the level of service. Salary varies depending on how many hours are worked and how much a bartender can make in tips. Bartenders can make a good deal of money depending on how busy the bar or restaurant is during a shift. Some bartenders work part-time as bartenders and have other jobs during the day. For others, bartending can be a full-time job. However, the hours are usually not regular working hours. Instead, most shifts are on nights and weekends. Some bartenders work at two different bars, working part-time at each. Other bartenders work at a bar part-time and have another bartending job working for a caterer or at special events like weddings or big parties.

ASK THE BARTENDER

Customers often ask bartenders for recommendations and other advice. They might want to know where the closest movie theater is or which nearby restaurant has the best steak. If customers are from out of town, they might want to know about local museums or sporting events. Therefore, a good bartender knows more than just how to make a particular drink. He or she must also know a good deal about the neighborhood and city. Customers sometimes might even ask for help with personal problems, like difficulties with a family member. Some bartenders joke that they are part bartender, part therapist.

The job of a wine director is not always full-time. It can often be a part-time job, and some wine directors work other jobs in the wine business. For example, they may work as a wine director at a hotel restaurant and as a special events coordinator for a winery. Salary varies based on how many hours are worked and the location. There are more opportunities for wine directors in cities, but wine directors can work all over the world.

chapter 6

MANAGERS

Many restaurants, cafés, and other dining establishments have a manager. Managers make the business side of a restaurant or other eatery run smoothly. The type of manager can vary depending on the size and number of employees. Larger restaurants, cafeterias, or chain restaurants may have a general manager. These employees are in charge of all business aspects of the restaurant. They manage all the other employees, order food and other supplies, pay employees, and keep track of the money made and spent by the restaurant.

Some restaurants also have a dining room manager. This person focuses on the "front of the house" and hires and manages servers, runners, bussers, hosts or hostesses, and reservationists.

Smaller restaurants, cafés, diners, or coffee shops may have a manager who also has many other duties in addition to managing. For example, one person may be the owner, head chef, and manager.

Any of these types of manager need to have a variety of skills. Managers must be very organized because they have many duties and have to keep track of lots of details. Managers must also be very good with people. They must manage not only the restaurant employees but may have interactions with customers as well. Managers are responsible for making sure customers are happy and have a positive dining experience.

Good business skills are necessary for managers as well. Managers keep track of all the money coming into the restaurant and often take the money to the bank. They also take care of all the money that is spent by the restaurant. This includes money for food, beverages, plates, cooking supplies like pots and pans, equipment like dishwashers and stoves, napkins and silverware, and cleaning supplies and services. Managers also

Managers often juggle many different duties, such as keeping track of the restaurant's wine list using a tablet computer.

keep track of each employee's hours worked and then pay employees, usually at the end of each week.

Managers must be flexible and resourceful. They need to be able to think on their feet to solve problems that may arise. For example, the dishwasher may break down during the busiest dinner hour. Or the chef may discover that one of the main ingredients for a popular menu item has spoiled. It is the

A manager's day often begins long before the restaurant opens, performing tasks such as checking food shipments from suppliers and ordering new supplies.

manager's job to find quick solutions to these and other problems.

Most managers work long hours because they need to be on-site while the restaurant is open. Often they are also there before the restaurant opens and after it closes. In dining establishments open seven days a week, managers may work every day of the week. In some cases, managers have assistants who help cover part of the time.

Some general managers, especially in large restaurants or in big hotels, have an assistant general manager. These employees help out in many aspects of the general manager's job. Some assistant managers handle specific tasks, such as payroll. Others help out as necessary with many or all of the general manager's job duties. Assistant general managers can fill in for the general manager during vacations or when the general manager is sick. Some also regularly help cover some hours. For example, the assistant general manager might

HOSTS, HOSTESSES, AND RESERVATIONISTS

Dining establishments with large or especially busy dining rooms sometimes employ hosts and hostesses or reservationists. Hosts and hostesses greet guests and take them to their table. They keep track of which tables are full so that servers will have an equal number of tables. They answer questions for diners and sometimes take money or credit cards at the end of the meal. Not all restaurants take reservations, but some that do hire reservationists. These employees answer calls from diners who would like to eat at the restaurant at a specific time. The reservationist tells diners whether tables are available and helps customers find other open times if a table is not available at the requested time. In some restaurants, hosts and hostesses might handle reservation duties. In others, the dining room manager may also act as host or hostess and reservationist.

work Sundays so that the general manager can have a day off. Also, an assistant might close up the restaurant a few nights a week.

JOB DESCRIPTION

A general manager is in charge of every aspect of a restaurant or other food service operation. The general manager hires chefs, other kitchen staff, servers, bartenders, and other employees. General managers sometimes also train new employees. They teach the new employees about the job and about the restaurant. The general manager also makes sure staff members are doing their jobs well. If someone is not doing a good job, the general manager must help him or her do better. In some cases, managers will have to fire employees.

Making up the work schedules for all employees is another task of the general manager. When an employee is sick or doesn't show up for work, the general manager must find a replacement. Sometimes the manager must fill in for absent employees, so he or she needs to know how to do the jobs of all staff members.

Some general managers also order all the food and other ingredients needed to make every dish on the menu. This includes all meat, vegetables, eggs, and other main essentials; spices, flour, and sugar for baking bread and desserts; milk for ice cream and sauces; and all beverages and liquor. General managers must make sure there is enough of every ingredient

A degree in accounting can be an invaluable asset for someone looking to make his or her way up in the restaurant industry.

in stock at all times. Some ingredients may be hard to find, so general managers must track down sources for these items.

In addition to ordering food supplies, general managers must order every other kind of supply that a dining establishment needs. For example, tablecloths, napkins, silverware,

In addition to basic courses such as accounting, a restaurant management degree program might include classes on restaurant design, motivating employees, and controlling costs.

plates, and glassware are needed for the dining room. The chefs need sharp knives, pots, pans, spoons and ladles, containers for holding food, and bowls for mixing. Appliances like stoves and ovens, refrigerators and freezers, dishwashers, and special equipment like mixers are also the responsibility of general managers. The general manager must purchase this equipment and know who to hire to fix it if it breaks.

The general manager is also responsible for keeping the restaurant clean. This includes supervising employees doing daily cleaning of the dining room, kitchen, and other rooms in the restaurant like bathrooms and stockrooms. The general manager also sometimes hires cleaning crews to do things like wash windows and shampoo carpets.

Some large restaurants or other dining establishments have a dining room manager. This person runs the "front of the house," or dining room. This sometimes also includes the bar. The dining room manager hires, trains, and manages the staff who work in the dining room. Servers, runners, bussers, hosts and hostesses, reservationists, and bartenders would work for a dining room manager.

In addition to supervising the dining room staff, dining room managers are responsible for keeping customers happy. He or she might walk around the dining room to greet customers and ask about their meals. A good dining room manager will remember regular customers and make them feel at home. Resolving problems with food or service is also part of a dining room manager's job. Handling special customer requests may be part of the job as well. For example, a diner may ask ahead for a type of food that is not on the menu. Or a customer may ask for help planning a special event like a birthday dinner or marriage proposal.

JOB PREPARATION

In most cases, a specific degree is not required in order to become a general manager or dining room manager. However, a business degree from a two- or four-year college can be a good idea. A bachelor's or associate's degree in management is another option for candidates to pursue. Yet another option is to attend a hospitality school.

There are certification programs specifically designed for restaurant managers. While these are not required, they can be a good idea for those who would like to become managers.

Taking classes in accounting and business is a good idea for any aspiring manager. Experience with computers is essential, as many restaurants use computers to track their inventory or to do payroll. Learning a second language, such as Spanish or French, can be very helpful. Some chefs and other kitchen workers may come from other countries and speak limited English.

While education and a good business background are helpful, management experience is key. Some restaurant managers work their way up from other jobs within a restaurant. For example, an aspiring manager could start as a server, move on to become a hostess, then dining room manager, and eventually the general manager.

Restaurant experience can be helpful, but management experience of any kind can be important. Even experience in an unrelated field, such as retail, can be helpful. Any previous job as a manager will help a candidate develop experience managing employees, dealing with customers, and other related business skills.

One of the best ways to train for a position as a general manager is to work as an assistant general manager. This position allows someone to learn all aspects of the manager's job.

SALARY AND ADVANCEMENT

Some restaurant employees, such as servers or dishwashers, earn an hourly wage. Managers are usually paid a yearly salary instead. This means they make the same amount whether they work twenty hours or fifty hours per week. Salaries for managers vary, depending on the size and type of dining establishment. Salaries can also vary depending on a manager's duties. In general, managers with more duties may make a higher salary. Managers of large, busy restaurants usually make more than those who work in smaller eating establishments.

Managers usually have good prospects for advancement. It is possible to work up from a lower-level position to become a general manager. General managers can move to other restaurants to advance their career. Or they can move to a different field. For example, a general manager of a restaurant may go on to become a general manager of a large hotel or resort.

glossary

apprentice An assistant to a skilled worker whose intention is to learn the trade.

back of the house Describing jobs in restaurants that are performed out of sight of the dining customers. These jobs usually include chefs, line cooks, and dishwashers.

caterer A person or business that supplies food and other services for a special event.

commercial Of or relating to commerce.

culinary Of or related to cooking.

externship A training program that takes place outside of school.

fixed schedule A schedule where one works the same hours every week.

flexible schedule A working schedule that can be adjusted to accomodate the needs of the restaurant or of the employee.

garnish A decoration or seasoning, usually applied to fine dishes.

internship A job that is often designed as an extension of one's education.

mousse A light, whipped dessert.

payroll The collective salaries of the employees of an establishment.

persuasive The ability to convince someone of something.

public relations The business of creating positive feedback for a person, establishment, or company.

salary Payment to an employee for his or her services.

sauté The practice of frying a food in a small amount of oil or butter.

shift A specified period of time during which an employee works.

vocational school A school that specializes in educating students in specific areas of employment.

volunteering The act of working for charity or to help others instead of for profit.

for more information

American Culinary Federation (ACF)
180 Center Place Way
St. Augustine, FL 32095
(800) 624-9458
Web site: http://www.acfchefs.org
The ACF is a top professional chefs' organization in North America. It hosts national events and offers certification and apprenticeship programs.

Canadian Culinary Federation (CCF)
30 Hamilton Court
Riverview, NB E1B 3C3
Canada
(506) 387-4882
Web site: http://www.ccfcc.ca
The CCF is a professional organization for chefs and other kitchen workers in Canada.

Culinary Institute of America
1946 Campus Drive
Hyde Park, NY 12538
(845) 452-9600
Web site: http://www.ciachef.edu
The Culinary Institute of America is one of the best-known culinary schools in the world. It has several locations and offers help to graduates looking for jobs in the culinary arts.

Institute of Culinary Education (ICE)
50 West 23rd Street
New York, NY 10010

(212) 847-0700
Web site: http://www.iceculinary.com
The ICE offers training programs in culinary arts, pastry
and baking, culinary management, and hospitality
management.

National Restaurant Association
2055 L Street NW
Washington, DC 20036
(202) 331-5900
Web site: http://www.restaurant.org
This is the leading restaurant association. Its Web site features facts and figures about the industry and has career
information.

National Restaurant Association Education Foundation
175 West Jackson Boulevard, Suite 1500
Chicago, IL 60604-2814
(800) 765-2122
Web site: http://www.nraef.org
The Education Foundation of the National Restaurant Association
features a program called Pro-Start, a two-year education and
work program available to high school students in most states
and U.S. territories.

Restaurant Opportunities Centers United
350 7th Avenue, Suite 1504
New York, NY 10010
(212) 243-6900
Web site: http://wwwrocunited.org
The mission of Restaurant Opportunities Centers United is to
advocate for fair wages and safe working conditions for the
nation's restaurant workers.

Union Square Hospitality Group
24 Union Square East, 6th Floor
New York, NY 10003
(212) 228-3585
Web site: http://www.ushgnyc.com
The Union Square Hospitality Group is the highly successful restaurant chain run by Danny Meyer. Located in downtown New York City, it is renown for such restaurants as the Union Square Cafe and Shake Shack.

WEB SITES

Due to the changing nature of Internet links, Rosen Publishing has developed an online list of Web sites related to the subject of this book. This site is updated regularly. Please use this link to access the list:

http://www.rosenlinks.com/ECAR/Rest

for further reading

Brefere, Lisa M., Karen Eich Drummond, and Brad Barnes. *So You Are a Chef: Managing Your Culinary Career*. Hoboken, NJ: John Wiley & Sons, 2009.

Chalmers, Irena. *Food Jobs: 150 Great Jobs for Culinary Students, Career Changers and Food Lovers*. New York, NY: Beaufort Books, 2008.

Crabtree, Marc. *Meet My Neighbor the Chef*. New York, NY: Crabtree Publishing Company, 2009.

Crabtree, Marc. *Meet My Neighbor the Restaurant Owner*. New York, NY: Crabtree Publishing Company, 2009.

Greathouse, Lisa. *Sweet: Inside a Bakery*. Huntington Beach, CA: Teacher Created Materials, 2011.

Gregory, Josh. *Chef*. North Mankato, MN: Cherry Lake Publishers, 2011.

Hill, Kathleen Thompson. *Career Opportunities in the Food and Beverage Industry*. New York, NY: Ferguson, 2010.

Kishel, Ann-Marie. *Server*. Minneapolis, MN: Lerner Classroom, 2007.

Kitazawa, Yuko. *Career Diary of a Pastry Chef*. Washington, DC: Garth Gardner Company, 2008.

Liebman, Dan. *I Want to Be a Chef*. Richmond Hill, ON, Canada: Firefly Books, 2012.

Mondschein, Ken. *Food and Culinary Arts*. New York, NY: Print Matters, 2009.

Rau, Diane Meachen. *Baker*. New York, NY: Benchmark Books, 2007.

Samuelsson, Marcus. *Yes, Chef*. New York, NY: Random House, 2012.

Smilow, Rick, and Anne E. McBride. *Culinary Careers: How to Get Your Dream Job in Food.* New York, NY: Clarkson Potter, 2010.

Thompson, Lisa. *Creating Cuisine: Have You Got What It Takes to Be a Chef?* Minneapolis, MN: CompassPoint Books, 2007.

bibliography

Brefere, Lisa M., Karen Eich Drummond, and Brad Barnes. *So You Are a Chef: Managing Your Culinary Career*. Hoboken, NJ: John Wiley & Sons, 2009.

Bureau of Labor Statistics, U.S. Department of Labor. "Bakers." *Occupational Outlook Handbook*, 2012–13 ed. Retrieved March 29, 2012 (http://www.bls.gov).

Bureau of Labor Statistics, U.S. Department of Labor. "Bartenders." *Occupational Outlook Handbook*, 2012–13 ed. Retrieved March 29, 2012 (http://www.bls.gov).

Bureau of Labor Statistics, U.S. Department of Labor. "Chefs and Head Cooks." *Occupational Outlook Handbook*, 2012–13 ed. Retrieved March 29, 2012 (http://www.bls.gov).

Bureau of Labor Statistics, U.S. Department of Labor. "Cooks." *Occupational Outlook Handbook*, 2012–13 ed. Retrieved March 29, 2012 (http://www.bls.gov).

Bureau of Labor Statistics, U.S. Department of Labor. "Food and Beverage Serving and Related Workers." *Occupational Outlook Handbook*, 2012–13 ed. Retrieved March 29, 2012 (http://www.bls.gov).

Bureau of Labor Statistics, U.S. Department of Labor. "Food Preparation Workers." *Occupational Outlook Handbook*, 2012–13 ed. Retrieved March 29, 2012 (http://www.bls.gov).

Bureau of Labor Statistics, U.S. Department of Labor. "Food Service Managers." *Occupational Outlook Handbook*, 2012–13 ed. Retrieved March 29, 2012 (http://www.bls.gov).

Chalmers, Irena. *Food Jobs: 150 Great Jobs for Culinary Students, Career Changers and Food Lovers.* New York, NY: Beaufort Books, 2008.

Hill, Kathleen Thompson. *Career Opportunities in the Food and Beverage Industry.* New York, NY: Ferguson, 2010.

Kitazawa, Yuko. *Career Diary of a Pastry Chef.* Washington, DC: Garth Gardner Company, 2008.

Mondschein, Ken. *Food and Culinary Arts.* New York, NY: Print Matters, 2009.

Samuelsson, Marcus. "About: Marcus Samuelsson." MarcusSamuelsson.com. Retrieved August 2, 2012 (http://www.marcussamuelsson.com/about).

Smilow, Rick, and Anne E. McBride. *Culinary Careers: How to Get Your Dream Job in Food.* New York, NY: Clarkson Potter, 2010.

Thompson, Lisa. *Creating Cuisine: Have You Got What It Takes to Be a Chef?* Minneapolis, MN: CompassPoint Books, 2007.

index

ABOUT THE AUTHOR

Simone Payment has a degree in psychology from Cornell University and a master's degree in elementary education from Wheelock College. She is the author of twenty-eight books for young adults. Her book *Inside Special Operations: Navy SEALs* won a 2004 Quick Picks for Reluctant Young Readers award from the American Library Association and is on the Nonfiction Honor List of Voice of Youth Advocates.

PHOTO CREDITS

Cover (waiter) Tad Denson/Shutterstock.com; cover (background), p. 1 Sergey Chirkov/Shutterstock.com; pp. 4–5, 52–53 Bloomberg/Getty Images; pp. 9, 11, 18–19, 21, 58–59 © AP Images; p. 14 Ethan Miller/Getty Images; p. 16 Ryan McVay/Photodisc/Thinkstock; p. 22 iStockphoto/Thinkstock; p. 24 Rick Wood/MCT /Landov; pp. 28–29, 63 The Washington Post/Getty Images; pp. 30–31, 50–51 Boston Globe/Getty Images; p. 33 Justin Sullivan/Getty Images; p. 36 Steve Baccon/Photodisc/Getty Images; p. 39 Jupiterimages/Creatas/Thinkstock; pp. 40–41 Top Photo Group/Thinkstock; pp. 42–43 Photofusion/Universal Images Group/Getty Images; pp. 46–47 © Napa Valley Register/ZUMA Press; p. 48 Steve Mason/Photodisc/Thinkstock; pp. 60–61 Ted Jackson/The Times-Picayune/Landov; pp. 64–65 Digital Vision/Getty Images.

Designer: Matt Cauli; Editor: Nicholas Croce;
Photo Researcher: Amy Feinberg